The Ten Books of
"I'LL TEACH YOU MY JOB!"

By Ken Tagawa

In Three 6x9 Volumes

Volume 1 — Books 1 through 4
"Struggling and Then... Magically Coming to Grips with Managing!"

Volume 2 — Books 5 through 8
"If You've Not Gotten the Results You Expected..."

Volume 3 — Books 9 and 10
"Revisiting Our Jobs So That We Ensure Astounding Success"

Table of Contents
Volume 1

"Struggling and Then... Magically Coming to Grips with Managing!"

A Commentary on How This Book Is Written. See the Appendix the end of Volume 3.

The List of All Ten Books

Book 1 — I Never Expected... Struggling, Magic, and BAM! Sudden Lightning Bolts!

Book 2 — What a Manager Has To Do... Subtraction and Get Rid of the Egregiously Bad

Book 3 — Connecting More Than Just Dots

Book 4.1 — Realizing What It Takes

Book 4.2 — Coming Together on Management

Book 5 — "Adults!" The Breakthrough to Managing Well

Book 6 — You Can't Change People, You Can Only Change the Way You Work with Them

Book 7 — The Book Specifically for Those of Us Who Are in Charge

Book 8 — The Twice-Weekly Meetings... Some Hold Them Every Day or Even Twice-a-Day

Book 9 — Teaching My Job!   A Revisit to Struggling, Magic, and BAM! Even More Lightning Bolts

Book 9.1 —Teaching My Job... Managing Themes and a Set of Current and Two New Activities

_____

Available in three other formats:

A softcover 6x9 edition with all 10 books.

A convenient 7-volume softcover print bookset, enabling each volume to be readily shared with your team, group.

Each volume is in an easy-to-carry, slimmer 5x8 slimmer format that slips into a personal bag/coat pocket.

And as an e-book.

Volume 1

ISBN: **9798657714333**

For you, the reader of this book...

This is a book to be used — *this is your book so* **make it your own!** *One of the first things you can do* — **write in it!** *Write your name/contact info on the cover or the back of the front cover.*

Also **write on the title page,**

> *"If you find this book, please return to me as this is an important book with information that really is meaningful to me!"*

Again, print your name, phone number, and write down the date!

Second: *To get the most out of this book, there are pages for notes at the end of each of the ten books. You are encouraged to use those pages to write your reactions, a thought to do something, or a reminder to share with your colleagues/group.*

You can use color pens or markers or pencils to circle, underline, or highlight any info so that info stands out! Draw arrows linking two things or cross-reference page numbers.

Third: *These thoughts/ideas to test, try out and share and perhaps develop into a new program or service — a new way of how things get done...* **are your "takeaways."**

While authors in many books summarize the takeaways for you at the end of a chapter, as I don't know your group or what you're responsible for, what I think really **isn't as important as what you come up with on your own!** *Your own takeaways are certainly going to be much more useful for you!*

Also, date whatever you write down. You'll be surprised at how the date – even where you were — when you thought of something will be a strong prompt that will powerfully remind you, perhaps even recommit you, so that your thought leads to something useful.

As you read this book, *you'll notice its layout is just different.*

This book is written in a **special "easy-to-read and quick to learn" layout.** *You'll see larger fonts, bolding of words and sentences for emphasis, unique line spacing...*

and changes in grammar and phrasing that would **cause your English teacher to just yell!**

"No! No! NO!!! That's totally unacceptable! You can't do that!!

I call this the "Tagawa Mastery Format" and you can read the Appendix — "A Commentary on How This Book Is Written" — at the end of this book and get an explanation how I came to write the book in this style/layout.

Want to know more about Ken Tagawa?

See his LinkedIn Profile.

Book 1 — "I Never Expected... Struggling, Magic, and BAM! Sudden Lightning Bolts!"

Continued from the Introduction

So, one day, I sat back and it just hit me...

Was I managing and leading? Hardly, I was struggling. I felt like I was pushing a wet noodle.

Can you manage and lead if you really don't know much about what's going on — what people are working on?

Of course not, but there I was, trying to manage and lead when **I didn't have a decent grasp** as to what everyone was doing...

I felt frustrated and stupid at the same time, but I also knew **I needed to somehow get that grip...**

So, the first thing I tried was the standing meeting every day.

We had been meeting once every two weeks and to now meet EVERY DAY was an abrupt change and... **people couldn't believe they had to stand while we met!**

But we weren't meeting just to be meeting. **In every meeting I started asking** what people were working on...

And out of that, over the days and weeks, came a huge list of what each person was doing, had to do,

but also a surprising number of things that I knew nothing about... **but nonetheless had to be taken care of.**

So, our meetings became not just, "What are you doing today and tomorrow and the rest of this week?"...

They become "What do you have to do this month and next month and the month after that"...

until finally we had a whole year — the full cycle of things we had to do, of deadlines... of preparation and organizational activities.

So, we knew much better which materials to develop, the events and meetings to schedule, and also the mailings to send out.

And as we all knew the tasks to make this all happen... **not only did we now know** who would be taking on the tasks that had to be done, we also knew the follow-up that would assure that we were doing everything we needed to do.

Of course, while **this was exhausting for everyone,** it was also exhilarating!

You could see the spark ignite!

They were hearing for the first time what each other was doing!

But they did dread coming to the next day's meeting because they knew **they'd be asked** if they had done what they said they had to do the previous day.

With unexpected interruptions and crises —

phone calls, urgent drop-ins from employees and managers, having to be out of the office for a doctor's appointment,

a meeting at your kids' schools or other personal/family concerns...

or being at meetings that lasted longer than scheduled and so on,

no one was always getting everything done...

They did revolt a bit, so we went to meeting twice a week — Tuesday and Thursday morning first thing and instead of standing...

I relented and we also all did sit — around a four-sided square meeting table.

Then something magical started to happen...

Somebody would talk about something they didn't get done or were working on...

something that was going on and had been brought to their attention, or a problem they had encountered.

And someone else would say,

"Oh, I know something about that," or, "That same person came to see me," or, "I had that same thing come up."

And Jerelle and Sharice would connect... **and piece together** the puzzle and come up with a better approach and solution.

Eventually it became obvious that those not at the meeting — the receptionist, the records clerk, a technical staff member also knew something.

16

But we didn't know they did until their managers went back to give them a debrief about the meeting they had been in with me...

and those who had not been in the meeting would say they knew something about that problem or issue.

They said enough things with enough of a different slant **that showed us that we** were working with incomplete information — that we didn't fully know what was going on.

So "Click!" — the light went on...

and I threw out the organizational chart — and nearly caused a revolution among the managers in the office.

The receptionist wasn't going to report to my assistant?

The benefits tech wasn't going to report to the benefits manager?

The compensation specialist wasn't going to report the employment manager?

And so on...

No one, I repeat, **no one had ever done that**... and just who were they going to report to?

Me!...

Me, because **I realized that I wasn't getting** the full picture.

Communication wasn't flowing — important information was getting lost in translation from one person to another or not surfacing at all.

And I knew that **without that full picture,** I as well as everyone working in our group would not fully know what was going on... and who was doing what.

And because we didn't know, we would continue to make mistakes... and there would be continued delays in getting things done.

Yes, whether it's the office or group I was in charge of or it's your team or unit or your leadership group, can any of us really say, who reports to whom and the layers we have is the best way to get things done?

While beyond the scope of this book, we've all assumed that the way we're structured is the "best way."

But given the number of times things don't quite come together or some important work doesn't get done, it's not unreasonable to question whether we're really organized the "best way."

So, **not by any grand design,** but because everyone ended up reporting to me, we became a flat organization — at the time when no one knew what a flat organization was!

And unexpectedly **the dynamics of the office** changed amazingly...

Managers who at first didn't like losing the people who reported to them... **suddenly found that they liked** not having that responsibility for supervising someone else's work.

However, they didn't like not being able to dump (I mean assign...) a difficult or boring matter onto someone else because that problem was now theirs and theirs alone.

Well, it **wasn't quite true** that it was theirs alone.

What happened again, magically but on a greater scale, was that when they talked about the problem, others — including those who previously reported to the manager

and who oftentimes wouldn't speak up out of deference or to avoid coming across as challenging their manager's view —

began speaking up and sharing what they knew and then pitched in to solve the problem.

And we really started to evolve more complete/whole pictures of the problems and then craft really fitting solutions!

And **the managers changed** also — that is, those who had been managers (they were no longer managers of people but managers of programs)...

learned not to direct, but to ask for help... asking if others knew about this problem or situation,

and that simple act of asking for help **changed the climate** of the office and —again, nearly magically — it felt like it happened overnight...

our work relationships **changed from hierarchical and directive... to collegial, collaborative, and communicative!**

All good for sure!

We're making a lot of positive progress... getting on top of things — the daily operational stuff and I knew much better what was going on,

---

but just because we had had a little success, we **couldn't get complacent...**

There was much more... And what was that "much more?"

Ask any manager, any supervisor or executive,

ask any employee...

and they'll tell you about the stuff that makes coming to work not such a great experience... stuff that makes their stomachs churn and their heads hurt...

They will tell you about stuff that you and they carry home every night it seems...

_____

that keeps you and them awake and perhaps a bit hesitant about coming to work the next day,

or perhaps even causing you/them to want to look for another job.

And even though everyone knows about these issues/challenges, they're tough and nobody is really ready to take them on...

to do something to take care of these issues, problems, or situations.

So, even though we were better and as much as I/we felt were had made amazing progress and liked getting on top of what we were doing...

certain things beyond the operational **wouldn't go away.**

These situations/challenges happened in my group... and through conversations with numerous others who were also managers or supervisors or executives,

it was clear that everyone was facing these challenges as well.

And what were these challenges?

These are the knotty things that go on between/among people in offices — sometimes work-related but which were also interpersonal interactions...

and on some occasions with those to whom they report — which means us!

We kept hearing about them — but I was so busy and we were so busy as a group trying to fix the operational...

that we didn't have time to think about them, much less do something to fix them.

But they don't go away... they just **don't go away.**

And as these problems kept popping up, they reminded us that we had other business — important business to take care of that required my attention.

So, as much as I'd like to tie up this first book by going back and sharing what we had accomplished and that we felt good about what we had done...

as much as we had unexpectedly/surprisingly turned things around and felt that we were not only doing good things but were really **moving in the right direction...**

as much sense as it made to think that we should build on

what we had done and move on/focus on our next positive steps,

I knew that so long as these difficult, long-neglected situations, involving egregiously bad people were allowed to exist in our groups, teams, and offices,

we clearly had challenges that now had to be taken care of.

Page for Notes

Page for Notes

Page for Notes

Book 2 — What a Manager Has to Do... Subtraction and Get Rid of the Egregiously Bad

Subtraction? Really?

As a manager or executive — and for sure as an employee, we absolutely know these egregious, gut-wrenching problems exist and **continue to** plague us!

And what's even worse, as we also know no one is doing much about them... that it's rare that anything is done about these folks,

and as you may also feel that you **can't do much** either, it shouldn't come as a surprise that these individuals with their bad attitudes and bad behaviors...

are just problems that **we have resigned ourselves** to putting up with.

So, what that leads us to think, even though these people — not just employees but also administrators and executives — make my stomach churn,

is that, as I don't also need to make the situation worse by taking on these people...

and as long as **whatever is going on** is tolerable and I can put up with it,

I don't need the headache that would undoubtedly happen if I took them on.

While some of us might **think it's reasonable** to handle these situations this way because doing so gets us through the day, the problem is... what if it isn't tolerable? What if one of these people says or does something that is completely unacceptable?

In the back of your mind, you know — as things aren't getting better and are likely getting worse,

that day is coming where you will have to do something.

Because the consequence is that, if you don't do anything, without any question, your inaction **will undermine you and keep you trapped** in an intolerable situation.

For me, I was somewhat surprised when I came up against these kinds of people and problems.

But knowing that I wanted to do a good job and to be highly effective... and **I also believe that most of us** also want to do a great job at work...

_____

the thought of having to put up with these people was simply unacceptable to me.

Thus, I found myself spending many hours trying to figure out how to deal with them. And one day, again, I had that **BAM experience!**

And it came to me... what I had to do.

"What simply came into my mind was a single word,

"SUBTRACTION"

SUBTRACTION? Why subtraction...

Because this word — which most of us never think of using,

told me/tells you **how to break out** and end the feeling that I was/you were "locked into" these unacceptable people.

And once you realize that **you also can get rid** of those who were causing these intolerable situations,

just like I experienced things turning around, I believe that you also will not only become much more effective...

you may even find yourself waking up and actually **looking forward** to coming to work!

So, "Subtraction" leads you to act!

Repeat: You can act — whether you're a manager, a supervisor, or an executive.

I know you can... because I did it... I did it when I was a manager without a lot of experience and had to deal with these egregiously bad people and difficult situations!

(And what and how I and those who worked with and for me were able to do this will be discussed later in this Book.)

Will taking action be worth it?

Absolutely!

Because... once you've taken care of these problems... by getting rid of these people or **putting them in their place —**

your office, team, or workgroup will also stop having those gut-wrenching knots in their stomachs... and, best of all...

because they know that what's unacceptable was handled by you...

you will be also be seen as amazingly more effective!

So, let's turn to examples of these egregiously bad people/situations — what we've called for years, **"the big dead moose."**

And whether you have some of them or all of them or even more, we're going to deal with them and "kick those dead moose off the table!"

Where to start:

While we were a diverse office, others were not... and

supervisors and managers had **paralyzing racial climate** issues.

In other units, supervisors were **being abusive, yelling** at employees,

and we had a bunch of allegations about discrimination and harassment.

There were also incidents of **workplace violence...**

But that's not all...

People were told to work overtime — being told to come in for evening or weekend events beyond the workday when they didn't want to... and they weren't being paid.

Then we **had instances** where people were getting overtime pay who shouldn't have... because their boss thought they were underpaid but couldn't get them promoted.

While this may not seem important... none of us really knew how to bring a new person on board.

We just assumed that people come to work to do a job... which is the way most of us think about work.

That is, working was a job for which you got hired to do certain things and few of us when we come on board have any sense that there might be something more.

But if we **want a better group** as well as to be part of a business/organization to work in and for... a place where people would want to work...

we had to raise the bar.

We had to convey somehow what we as a group and this organization stood for — so that people could understand... why, beyond a paycheck, should they want to work here?

As I said in Book 1, because we weren't on top of what we were doing — because we were making too many mistakes and spending so much time fixing what we had messed up,

we were so consumed with trying to get the day-to-day stuff done that... we didn't have time or energy left to deal with these problems.

However, once we began to get our operational house in order, **we were freeing** up our time, and could begin to think about taking on and dealing with these pervasive long-neglected problems.

So, with the backdrop of knowing about all of these challenges, it would have been easy for me — as the person "in charge" —

to put together a plan — a "strategic plan" —

something you can also do or may have already had experience doing...

with a set of operational priorities focused on these problems.

But being effective is not about planning. It's about **doing something** and doing the right something!

So, because it was critical to get this right, rather than doing what a manager would normally do — crafting that plan and putting it out there to solicit input and feedback,

I got struck by a lightning bolt!

We had had success in the operational stuff...

because we got on top of what we had to do by involving everyone so that we could understand what we were doing and therefore how best to get organized.

Could we do something similarly to take on these long-standing challenges?

And as **I began to raise** these egregious problems, and just as I had come to know that everyone knew the problems in our operational work,

it was no surprise that they – like Fiona and Damon – also knew about and had experience with these challenges.

Yet even though we had had amazing success where magically everything came together to solve our operational problems and...

while it was reasonable therefore to assume that we could also take on these problems, somehow these **challenges were going to be different.**

Taking on these long-standing problems —

these terrible egregious problems —

the huge dead moose that everyone saw but no one had done anything about for years...

was not the same as fixing operational problems and figuring out processes.

These were **simply different, something more...**

And as we talked, what we came to realize is that **these problems were about** the nature of who we were and our organization,

and that taking on these problems meant we were going to have to face one of the biggest challenges in any business or organization — which was to **change the culture.**

And, as the key to changing the culture was having everyone know what the organization stood for...

we knew we had to send a message that those who were the badly egregious would know that **they'd have to change or move on.**

GETTING STARTED:

Just as we had gone through the "what did we have to do today, tomorrow, this week, month and year"… to get our operational responsibilities in order,

We sought to **get that grasp** for taking on these organizational issues…

and embarked on a strategic planning retreat so that we would understand, get organized and do what was needed to take on these problems.

We did the usual approach to a strategic plan which is to do an environment scan —

a huge brainstorm and put everything up — over a hundred items…

on the board for all of us to see what could possibly be of concern to us or impact us or the people working in the organization.

As we did this exercise... it was not surprising to see that these long-standing **"dead moose" problems kept popping** up in various forms and situations.

But while the magnitude of the issues was a bit unnerving... how could things have gotten this bad?

it was good that we could begin to see clearly what we faced.

What followed then was a SWOT analysis — **S**trengths, **W**eaknesses, **O**pportunities, and **T**hreats regarding these composite groupings...

where, in having nailed down as clearly as possible what we would need to take on,

we had to ask whether we had the capacity — the strength we could turn to and utilize to resolve these issues.

(I soon came to realize this concern was unwarranted which I'll explain later.)

I led the whole retreat for two days and, of course, it was exhausting for me and... frankly, the interest on the part of others waned noticeably and understandably at times.

But, as we came to understand these problems, as we began to see the outline of **what our future might be...**

a better-run organization — one where the wrong stuff that was going on would be minimized or stopped,

an organization where people would begin to see and begin to believe that things were getting better,

a place where people would begin to look forward to coming to work every day,

a place where the organizational climate was not going to stay what it had been for years but had begun to shift...

---

our optimism grew and we came away with a sense that we did have a shot at changing the culture!

WHAT DID WE TAKE ON FIRST?

As I said, this was not about planning, but acting to take care of these problems.

Right off the bat, we knew we had to stop the stuff that everyone knew about, but nobody had done anything about —

leave abuse, people coming into work late and leaving early and taking two hours for lunch...

and we had to fix the overtime problems.

But we also knew **we had to stop abusive workplace behavior...**

We had to end the feeling that these egregiously bad employees, these just unquestionably difficult people for whatever reason —

as well as bad supervisors and managers would **never be dealt with.**

This didn't necessarily mean firing people, but it did mean that — not just me, but you — whether you're a manager, a supervisor, a division head...

or an executive group member, even the president or the CEO,

had to immerse ourselves into the inner-workings of our offices and groups and to **change the work**

dynamics and relationships there.

We knew this had to be done.

It was bad enough that the "egregiously bad and difficult" employee, supervisor, or manager... was making their current colleagues unhappy and perhaps feeling hopeless about their work situation,

we had to recognize that **our allowing workplace abuse** to continue would also mean that any people we had hired —

once they started to work and then saw the internal problems of the workplace and what was not being taken care of,

some of them would not only have question their decision to join us... some might also then decide to leave because of the climate/culture...

And...

all the work we had done, the efforts we had made to bring in better people — new colleagues we had worked hard to join us — would be for naught.

But, while we realized that **it was imperative** to get at each instance of the bad/difficult employee, manager, or supervisor problem,

it was obvious that the problem of workplace abuse was not limited to a few isolated cases...

that the approach of responding to and "fixing" each specific problem after it had occurred was like a game of **organizational "whack a mole."**

And as we were always playing "catch-up" — it became very clear that trying to deal with these egregiously bad people and situations this way was not going to work in the long-run...

and would not lead to enduring change that would make us a better organization.

Thus, **rather than being reactive,** we realized that, if we wanted to make our organization better, what we needed an organization-wide solution...

one that was proactive.

And, without any forethought, what we found ourselves saying in doing the SWOT analysis at the retreat... was that all these problems which were repeatedly occurring...

were things we didn't like... because they were violations of our personal values and...

BAM!

what some of us knew... were also totally counter to what we say in policies and manuals about who we were to be!

That is, as in any organization, we **said the right things...**

      treat each other with respect, value our diversity and multi-culturalism,

be collaborative and supportive, and conduct ourselves with professionalism.

So it wasn't that these statements — these ideas and principles didn't exist. They did, but what had happened was that as an organization...

we had let lapse/never clearly established that these statements were what was expected of people in the workplace...

As an organization, we just **had a big hole...**

that, even though policies which should back, support, and encourage every employee, every manager, and every supervisor, every division head, and those who were executives...

across the entire organization to **do the right thing,**

our problem really was that these policies which were "on the books" — found in manuals and numerous memoranda —

had long been **"in effect but never enforced."**

I know your reaction...

Policies? Really? Enforce?

I understand that most people, including anyone reading this book, understandably can be skeptical about policies and their impact.

Far too often, our experience is that policies often "just get in the way of getting things done"... but policies, in these cases of the egregiously bad stuff,

were just logical and were what was needed...

In fact, **they were exactly what was needed!**

That is, policies — unequivocally clear statements of the organization's values and expectations...

would reinforce and strengthen the behaviors and attitudes

that should just be the way things are in a decent, productive place to work.

It also became clear that unless everyone,

including executives as well as managers, supervisors, and those in our group –

as well as anyone else wherever s/he might work in the organization,

became aware of these policies... and to know the expectations that they should adhere to, the problems of bad/difficult employees, managers, supervisors, and executives would remain.

It came down to the fact that getting better **wasn't a matter of courage —**

of feeling so aggrieved or insulted by bad behavior and attitude that one finally had to speak up and act.

Getting better — changing the culture to get rid of the egregiously bad and to make us a better place to work...

was simply a matter of consistently stating what were desired workplace norms and values,

and then to act... which was what policies enabled us to do!

That is, while they were reflective of legal requirements, policies were really statements of the ideals of the organization.

And as statements of expectation that could be enforced...

policies would not only express what the culture of our organization should be... and thus influence and affect what was going on in various offices and between/among people,

creating not just a decent but hopefully a highly desirable place to work.

They were also the basis to help us to remove/"subtract" or put the difficult, egregiously bad individuals in their place where their adverse attitudes and behavior would be limited/stopped.

So, we figured out which policies needed to be issued or rewritten… and keep in mind, every organization, every business has statements like these!

and we crafted new policies that were needed to take on these issues.

We put out a notice tied to the organization's fraud policy… and brought to everyone's attention… that anyone who was not reporting his/her sick leave and vacation leave correctly was committing fraud —

a criminal offense that might possibly lead to termination of employment and/or that the organization might choose to prosecute.

That was followed by **a "zero tolerance"** policy on workplace violence... a new policy — not to encompass just physical violence (assaults), but also psychological violence...

that **toxic, intolerable stuff** that makes people's stomach churn...

intimidation, speaking angrily/openly yelling at someone that some people just, for whatever reason —

perhaps their crazy notion of how to manage and lead because they were in charge, **chose to inflict** on others...

but in doing so, by behaving this way, they were making for a place where no one would want to work/would dread coming to work.

To deal with **the problem of people coming** into work late or leaving early, we sent out a memorandum reiterating the policy on organizational workhours (8 to 5).

And this workhours policy gave us the leverage to address the overtime problem.

That memorandum on overtime went out to
managers/supervisors/executives and was also sent to those who work with and for you... to not ask/compel their employees —

who were on a 40-hour work week and eligible for overtime for hours worked beyond 40 hours,

to work beyond standard work hours.

Finally, I got myself as well as three others **trained to investigate incidents** and to deal with complaints.

By conducting these investigations, issuing findings, and making recommendations and tying the reports to policies,

while we took on and resolved the specific instances of discrimination and workplace violence...

and while we were letting everyone know for perhaps the first time what the organization's policies and institutional expectations were,

the real impact was the organization's **culture was changing.**

As we started taking on these long-standing adverse practices, there was remarkably very little objection or much comment about what we were doing.

After all, as everyone knew about these problems but with nothing being done for years,

why would anyone have any expectations that what we were doing would have lasting change, that anything would be different?

However, we **didn't have to wait** long for our first test.

The policy changes did catch some people's eye.

And one day, a courageous employee... who had transferred from another organization could not believe that her boss —

an executive — was regularly yelling at her and others in the office. This executive had been doing this for years and even though numerous "conversations" had been held, nothing changed.

When the workplace violence policy came out, this employee **asked for an investigation.**

I conducted the investigation... a report was issued and the administrator's behavior was found to be unacceptable... in violation of the zero-tolerance workplace violence policy.

No one said much of anything, but **the word spread.**

The leave abuse memorandum tied to the fraud policy also caught people's attention.

No one had thought that leave abuse was really fraud — a misrepresentation where someone was receiving undeserved financial benefit!

It wasn't long before we were told about a situation in a unit where the person was alleged to have failed to report vacation and leave usage for years.

In another instance, a couple of employees had taken extended time off (which was not reported) because they had worked long hours on a project.

Because the leave abuse was **tied to the organization's fraud policy,** internal audit which was responsible for issuing that policy got involved.

They conducted their investigation and issued their report, resulting in the dismissal of employees and a strong reprimand to the head of the unit.

Closer to home, I had one employee who resisted the work hour policy.

This individual would often come in late to work, dropping a child at school... and then take lunch at 11:30AM to avoid the lunch-time rush.

Leaving early for lunch was bad enough, but the person "on occasion" then didn't return to work until 1PM or later,

when everyone else on the one-hour lunch break schedule would come back to work.

I explained the policy, enforced it by not allowing the person to leave early for lunch and the person soon found another job.

As a result of these actions, **the word got out... amazing how fast the grapevine is.**

Even in the face of a long history of things not being done or taken on, people began to sense that these challenges that had long not been addressed were no longer acceptable.

And what we were after began to happen.

You could sense the **organizational climate beginning to shift...**

It really didn't take long...

That as the egregiously bad employee — whether an executive or a professional or a technical/support staff...

by our relying on policy to either remove — that is, to subtract these individuals or to put them in their place,

was no longer being allowed to "get away" with being abusive or not being held accountable, we were becoming that better place...

the kind of place that now had a culture where people would want to come to work.

Page for Notes

Page for Notes

Volume 1

Page for Notes

Book 3 — "Connecting More Than Just Dots"

Fast forward to the next year —

Operationally we've made a lot of progress — feeling pretty good about getting on top of our work...

and we've also started to successfully take on the "Dead Moose" stuff.

All pretty exciting and energizing!

We go on another retreat to step back and get perspective so we can figure out how to be better.

Now, I know we've all been on retreats, but what happened at **this retreat opened my eyes...**

and let me begin to see a number of things about those who worked with and for me that would make us even more effective.

We start with a team-building exercise where each of us tells our life history — what got each of us to where we are now and what were the events that helped shape our lives.

I watched in amazement as **people opened up —** they weren't just engaged in a team-building exercise. It was clear that everyone was interested in hearing about each other...

They wanted to know more about what made someone tick.

And as I watched, more than just a light bulb going on,
another lightning bolt struck!

Because I already knew from the work we had done on operational tasks and the schedule of daily work... as well as the calendar and the "dead moose" challenges...

that these are **clearly smart people.**

And now, from these conversations at the retreat about each person's background/what they had done, I realized that...

these are also people who, in their lives, are not waiting for someone to tell them what to do,

these are people who are **shaping their own lives!**

And on the spot, I decided that each person... would be responsible for a part of the retreat — and thus help shape what we were doing.

To get this underway, I emphasized to each of them that they should act like they were the director, that they **were now in charge** and each would have lead responsibility for running a portion of the retreat...

whether the environment scan, the SWOT analysis, or the determination of our priorities

to come up with the must do's and the really want to do's that we knew we had to develop!

Of course, **doing the retreat this way wasn't** even on the agenda, but after a few moments of hesitation...

"Are you sure? Is this really what you're going to have us do?"

Their reluctance was understandable... they had never been given the chance to be in charge at work... they were used to being told what to do and to react to someone else's ideas or thoughts.

But as it became clear that I was serious in wanting them to do this, people came out of their shells and they started to change.

In fact, some really jumped at the opportunity — and to be honest...

some like Lola expressed such strong opinions and recommendations — they shocked most of us with the directness of what they'd do (actually demand) in changing things.

But, as difficult as this was to run the retreat this way, **the light began to go on** in my head and I came to realize...

if we were to come up with what we needed to work on, it was critical to hear what people were really thinking... what they thought we should do.

Of course, with not all people being the same, as the various discussions proceeded,

those who had not spoken up initially... **found their voices** and asked questions that needed to be asked and shared powerful insights.

It was surprising to hear how much they knew... And then those who were usually more demanding and insistent that their point of view was right,

instead of ordering and trying to be in control (that is, "directing"), they did what they did in the daily meetings — what they knew had worked...

They began to share why they had a particular view, to ask for input, to seek out the thoughts and views of others.

And as they did this, the demanding ones came to realize that as a manager, "you really do have to get work done through others,"

and the others **responded positively and delivered!**

So, the retreat tells/helps us see what's not working operationally, and where we are on the egregiously bad "dead moose" challenges,

and that we have also begun to develop a sense of what to work on to make us as well as the organization better.

All of which, of course, was good...

But the best thing that came out of the retreat was that we learned... more like "had stumbled upon" —

that having each person lead a part of the retreat was a **"better way"** to pull out concerns and develop solutions to move us forward!

While what we did at the retreat was entirely new, and while we got a much better sense of what we had to take on, we also learned two other important things:

FIRST, what we came away with — drawn from the environment scan and the SWOT analysis... was not our goals, which is the standard outcome of strategic planning, but...

a solid list of important projects to work on.

These projects became our focus for change... "By the end of X — the calendar year, summer, three months, or whatever timeframe."

Grouping these projects together around the theme —
"What We Wanted to Look Like,"

we never even talked about goals! We only talked about what we needed to do to take us to the next level/something of desired change...

and by the end of the retreat, we knew these projects would also enable our office to further move the organization to a better place.

As I said, as a beginning manager, **I knew about goals** from previous strategic planning efforts,

but what these retreats — which we did every year thereafter to come up with the list of items of "What We Wanted to Look Like" —

did was to shift us to come up with what was really important... **"concrete deliverables!"**

We weren't spending our time and tying up our heads working toward some "pie-in-the-sky" goals... some aspirational vision of a future.

What we were working on… were things that would have direct, positive, and immediate impact on the daily work we had to do…

and also on what was going on in offices, with our colleagues, and across the organization.

So, we're **making huge strides operationally** because we're now working together collaboratively,

and we're also effective in taking on these long-standing egregious problems that would change the culture,

And now through the retreat we're creating those concrete deliverables that would provide a forward focus of change in the organization.

And when we came back to work, we put all of this into the calendar and daily schedule.

And we did so with the same structure —

> the full cycle of deadlines, preparation and organizational activities, materials to develop, events and meetings to be scheduled, mailings and communications

the tasks to make this all happen... as well as the follow-up to make sure we had done what we said we needed to do, and who was responsible for what.

And so that we would be reminded every day, we put all we had come up with — the "What We Wanted to Look Like" —

on the board in the common work area where we met **SO**

we could see them every day!

It was pretty surprising how things came together — how what had seemed disconnected had just become connected...

our roles and relationships, these projects for concrete deliverables... and how we organized ourselves now just fit together!

Of course, not surprisingly... just as how we ran the retreat had changed, **our meetings also changed.**

We not only had an expanded calendar/schedule with initiatives related to policy/culture/climate... we also had the addition of the "concrete deliverables" tied to items in the list of "What We Wanted to Look Like."

And seeing we had much more to take on, we also changed how we did our daily work —

changing our jobs to match our processes and to assure the efficient development of the initiatives and concrete deliverable projects.

And as we also all now knew what each other was doing — the full range of each other's work — and with everyone pretty much having the same or complementary jobs...

we were working so collaboratively that **we ended the handing-off** of work and the "dizzying whirligig" of moving documents from one person to another.

That is, with each person or a group being assigned as a point of contact and handling the work we were expected to do... for employees and managers in a set of offices or groups in a particular area of the organization...

we were no longer handing off work which minimized the delays caused by the fragmentation of work.

We also found that, as we no longer had the problem of losing paperwork, amazingly, things **abruptly stopped dropping** through the cracks!

We had simply become faster and better at getting done what had to be done!

We had connected a lot of dots — the operational, culture and policy, the challenges, the "What We Wanted to Look Like" and the concrete deliverables — and what we got was much more complete... whole pictures of what people wanted...

and what situations, problems, and challenges were occurring and what we had to take on to make things better in the organization.

As we were taking on a lot, to keep us on track with all we were working on as well as our daily work,

we brought on board the first multi-user relational database... and used it to track every piece of paper that came into our office.

We knew when the document came in and who it went to... who was working on what.

We also knew when something was passed on to someone else and who that person was and the disposition of the document.

Through all of this, not only did we come to know even better what each other was doing, we came to know how what each of us was doing fit together...

and nearly **magically to also support one another.**

And without much effort or difficulty, when someone was overburdened or was absent, it was easy for someone else to stand in and pick up each other's work nearly seamlessly.

And in doing so, we ended the complaints that had haunted this office for years — that we were incompetent, that we were losing things, that we didn't know what we were talking about and that we couldn't be trusted to do our jobs to serve our colleagues!

Again, all good, but best of all,

as important as the concrete deliverables and our working together and changing our image and the perception of our effectiveness was...

as a workgroup, we also got that SECOND insight which was something even more important.

What we brought back from the retreat... and as we reorganized how we did our work, we came to acknowledge/to realize with even more conviction that... **each person was fully capable of leading...**

and the twice-weekly meetings evolved to where each person would be in charge — just as we had done at the retreat — on a rotating basis

and would run these meetings around **our symbolically square table with no head!**

This capacity to lead — which was always there in each person — became a huge strength of the group!

None of this had happened because someone had a grand scheme — a plan or some notion of what a great operation or an office should look like...

or how a group of people could really make things happen.

For sure, **it happened because...**

I knew as the manager that the standard way of doing things,

an occasional staff meeting and "my being the person in charge"... and having the "authority to lead" from the typical list of manager responsibilities, was not working.

But it happened for other reasons as well.

It also happened because I had that vision of that group back in Tokyo where I had worked.

It happened because I was fortunate enough to **somehow wake up and realize** that the people I was working with were amazingly smart...

that because these were people who were shaping their own lives, and who knew their jobs better than I ever would,

that they would have the insight to enable them to make crucial contributions... to figure out and do what was necessary for us to be successful.

It happened because I realized...

that they knew the problems in their jobs that stymied what each person as well as what the group was being tasked to accomplish better than I ever would,

and that **they also knew the solutions...** but what they knew had never been tapped into before.

It happened because somehow that lightning bolt — which made me realize that everyone has the capacity to lead, something they had in their own personal lives —

also made me realize that I only needed to stop thinking I was solely responsible for being in charge...

and that they would **step up and deliver,**

In response to a problem, I would offer a solution and put it on the table.

Invariably people would come back with a different and better solution!

That they would come back with better solutions wasn't surprising. As they knew their jobs better than I would ever know, why shouldn't they have a better way?

And then, when they had finished explaining their better approach, they liked to say back to me something I had told them – a saying I learned in Japan,

"There are many ways to climb Mt. Fuji..." and we'd all laugh...

----

and would do so **with an amazing synergy** that made us all more effective and productive.

Again, having dealt with the operational, the egregiously bad, and developing a sense of the concrete deliverables, it would be easy to now also stop at this point.

Clearly the group had become highly effective...

and, while the development of each person's capacity to lead was essential to our daily work to continue to address the organizational challenges of culture and climate...

but now to also develop a much better sense of what our work ahead was going to be —

that is, the concerns falling into "What We Wanted to Look Like," to move our group, our division and even the organization really forward,

we realized that putting initiatives together and developing the concrete deliverables was not easy to do.

We realized that if we were to be successful... **doing so would take longer-range,** more complex and overarching thinking and organizing.

It meant we had to plan and to plan well, it meant... **we had to manage!**

We knew we had the capacity to lead — which happened through the retreat,

but if we —

including myself who began by struggling to figure out what I was to do in this job... what I would do as a manager —

and this group of people, most of whom really had not held formal management responsibilities —

now had to manage,

the obvious question that loomed... the question that needed answering was, were we ready?

95

Could we take what we knew from leading and managing/shaping our own lives and leverage that to move us forward at work?

Page for Notes

Page for Notes

Page for Notes

Book 4.1 — "Realizing What It Takes"

Developing a capacity to manage was critical since neither I nor those in our group had been managers who had been highly effective.

And now, with us as a group **striving to** develop concrete deliverables, there was no question...

that it was **imperative to figure out the best way to manage** to take on the work of developing these new initiatives.

This Book 4.1 and the following two books **are controversial. They depart from conventional wisdom...**

If you're an established manager, you might find some/considerable disagreement with what I write because, after all, you've been able to do your job of managing with decent if not solid results for a number of years.

I can't argue with that view.

However, I want to give you something to think about.

Just because the NY Yankees from the 30's to the 60's were world champions of baseball numerous times didn't mean that they would continue to be successful — to dominate the game of baseball.

In fact, we know they didn't. Other teams became quite good — Milwaukee, Boston, Baltimore, Brooklyn, Atlanta — and later Houston and Los Angeles as well as Chicago, St. Louis, and Cleveland regularly fielded highly competitive championship teams. The Yankees remained decently competitive but no longer dominant.

And why not? Was it possibly related to less than stellar management and leadership? Perhaps an organization that wasn't working quite right? Or decisions that were made which turned out to be not on target if not flat-out wrong? Or did they somehow stand still with what they thought was a proven formula while other teams changed and became outstanding?

And to get back to this book and our focus on businesses and organizations...

Keep in mind that only five companies of those that constitute the Dow-Jones Industrial Average were part of the Dow in 1975 — Exxon, Procter and Gamble, DuPont, United Technologies, and 3M. GE, the last member of the original DOW group, was dropped in 2018. Additionally, over 50% of the companies listed in the Fortune 500 have been replaced since the early 2000s.

Was management a factor in the decline/failure of those companies?

And as I'm pondering what to do, this guy named **ElRoy Face suddenly popped** into my mind!

Wow... total surprise! ElRoy Face??

What possible connection could ElRoy Face — a baseball pitcher in the 50's and 60's — have to our managing challenge?

But, as ElRoy Face wouldn't disappear from my thoughts, one afternoon, **it hit me!**

We all know that **some people** are great managers; however, we also know they are **few and far between.**

Then there are some/many of us who fall in the middle group. We're decent... we're ok... we do what we need to do to try to get the job done.

But for most of what we do, we're not extraordinary, and being in the middle group, it means **we're at best average...**

And, of course, there are a few of us who are struggling.

So, what does that have to do with ElRoy Face?

A lot...

As a minor league pitcher, ElRoy Face was quite successful.

Over five seasons, opposing teams were held to the equivalent of less than 4 runs per game...

and he compiled a won-lost record of 69 and 27, a winning percentage of 72% or nearly 3 out of every four games he pitched.

However, when he was brought up to the major league team, the Pittsburgh Pirates, for the 1953 season,

the hitters on the opposing teams were able to hit his pitching, and his run allowed per game average nearly doubled, rising to nearly 7 runs per game.

And during those first five years of his major league career with the Pirates, ElRoy Face was doing okay,

but his won-lost record fell to 32 wins and 36 losses, with a winning percentage of 47% or about average.

But **suddenly** in 1959, he did something that was simply extraordinary.

Unexpectedly... and **to the amazement** of the entire baseball world, a guy who had been a pitcher with an average record...

did the exceptional feat that no one else had done before!

ElRoy Face won 18 games and lost only one!

ElRoy Face started his major league career in 1953, but not with great success. And in his first season (1953) his RA9 (runs allowed adjusted to 9 innings) was 6.81. This means if he pitched a full nine innings, nearly 7 runs a game would be scored by the opposing team when he was the pitcher.

As this RA9 was too high, he was told to develop another pitch. So, in 1954, he developed the forkball...

And for the next six seasons (1955-1960) with Pittsburgh, he remarkably reduced his RA9 from nearly 7 to 4.15, 3.79, 3.94, 3.23, 2.80 (1959), and 3.06. Of note, in his career, he had five seasons when his RA9 was below 3.00.

In talking with ElRoy Face about his pitching prowess, he took particular pride in the fact that he had pitched in 9 straight games which is beyond what nearly any other pitcher could do! Because of the stress on their arms caused by the violent act of throwing the ball oftentimes upwards of 90 miles per hour, pitchers usually require at least two if not three days of rest to recover between the games they would pitch. Face pitched in 17 innings across those 9 games.

And in compiling **the best winning** percentage of 94.7% for a pitcher in the history of baseball,

he changed the way the game is played!

So how did Face go from being average to extraordinary?

Simple: He changed what he was doing as a pitcher... and threw the ball in a different way that no one else in major league baseball was doing...

And when Face threw his forkball, it was a pitch that most hitters found difficult to hit!

Of course, **Face captivated** the baseball world, **becoming known as the first "closer"** in the game of baseball...

a pitcher who would come into the game in the late innings to shut down the other team.

And by having such great success capped by his 18-win 1-loss season in 1959,

thus forcing other baseball teams to develop their own specialized relief pitchers to compete against him in the late innings of a baseball game,

ElRoy Face changed the way the game is played!

COMING TO GRIPS WITH MANAGING

So, nice story about ElRoy Face, but **what possible connection** does this have to do with managing?

The success of ElRoy Face tells us, whether we're a manager, a supervisor, a director, or an executive...

while there are reasons why we fall short and even fail at times...

there are also **things we can do to optimize** our chances of being successful!

And, as I thought about my own career and why I was a struggling manager, **I had some important breakthroughs**...

that led me to understand what wasn't working and helped put my head in the right place and what I had to change.

It started with... despite all we've read and been told,

the simple fact is that we're not trained for success... we're trained to be average.

Wait! Stop!

We're not trained for success? How did you come up with that?

I thought about the jobs I had held and I also talked with many others who were in management.

If you asked whether **the jobs we held** were the same as previous jobs we had, we all would say they were similar, but not the same...

different organizations, different businesses, different activities, different priorities, different responsibilities.

All true, but then I thought:

Even though the jobs were different, when any of us got into a new position, **did we bring** what we had done previously to our current jobs?

Of course!

No one starts anew. **We bring** what we thought worked in our previous jobs and try to use that in our new jobs!

So, then I thought, if we say that..."as a manager in a new job, most of us continue to use what we had used in our previous jobs..."

even though we all know that the problems aren't the same and the work as well as supporting systems/processes are not the same...

isn't that a problem?

In response people said,

Well, because the job is new, we know that we're going to **have to learn** some things about our new place of work if we're to be successful.

And again, as that made total sense...

I asked, "What did you do?   What did your organization or business do?"

Nearly everyone said that, as a new manager or supervisor, they got sent to a new manager or supervisor training session...

and some also got sent to a leadership development program (upper management, executives) that the organization had put together!

And when I asked, "What did you learn? Did you **find the session helpful?"**

People replied that, while there was some new information about the organization or the company,

these sessions — regardless of the organization or company — **were pretty much the same.**

Well organized, but they covered much of what we **already knew:**

a vision/mission that gave an overview, followed by information on hiring, performance management, communication, mentoring and coaching, and compliance.

So, because we've all gone through these programs at previous places we had worked and thus already know a lot about these topics,

I came to an important realization.

As there's nothing really new in these programs, **they don't make you better.**

And the reason they don't... is because the information/training being provided which all attending the workshop are expected to understand and use — is the same,

and **by targeting all managers** with the same content, these workshops simply can't be responsive to what you or I — as managers with **our unique situations, issues, and problems** — have to deal with!

And then that big, glaring light bulb went on!

What any manager really wants is the information I/you need to be effective in our work...

and in order to do that — in order to make a difference... to provide better service, faster and improved operations, to assure production of goods and products...

to create the conditions for stronger performance by everyone,

what we have to focus on... are the problems, issues, and challenges that are **unique to the work** we're doing!

Repeat! If we — meaning myself and those in my group — are to be effective,

what we have to focus on are the problems, issues, and challenges that are unique to the work we are doing!

For, if we handle those effectively, we will provide precisely what our customers and clients want and/or need!

If it were simply a matter of bringing what we'd done previously — and combining it with what we learned in training,

each time we took on a new position, **we'd build** on what we know, adding what we've just learned... and be on an **ever upward-moving path** of greater and greater success!

But we know that **ever-escalating success** doesn't happen... because what we've been told is not specific to the office or work group that we're in charge of.

And because we received the same information — information many of us already had and information that's not about the problems, issues, and challenges we have to take care of, we don't become better in the work we're responsible for.

And, since we just don't really improve, **I came to realize** that what these workshops do... in laying out what the organization expects of all managers,

is to pretty much bring everyone **to the same decent level** of management.

And thus, not only should we not be surprised that so many of us are just decent, average managers...

we also shouldn't be surprised that **we achieve similar level (meaning average) of results!**

And what directly follows is... because I and most of you were trained to be average,

and not sufficiently trained to manage and lead in handling the real problems and issues that I and those working with and for me had to deal with every day...

those daily operational problems and the egregious challenges of "bad employees, colleagues and administrators" within our offices or groups.

it should also not come as a surprise that I...

that many of us who are managers **would fall short...**

couldn't be superbly effective!

It was this realization through these conversations with many other managers about their careers — and also by reflecting on my own career…

that led me to understand that the standard approach to managing **won't achieve fabulous results.**

And, just like that… I suddenly understood — like ElRoy Face who understood that he had to change to pitch effectively,

why making a change — **a change, whether we're a baseball pitcher or a manager…**

to focus on what we had to do in our daily work...

is what's needed to enable us to be highly successful in all that we were undertaking!

Page for Notes

Page for Notes

Page for Notes

Book 4.2 — "Coming Together on Managing"

Once I realized that we were not being trained — whether formally or informally — to be extraordinary, that we weren't being trained for success,

I had another piece of **unconventional wisdom about managing** pop into my mind!

And this second perspective will seem a little strange...

I've just written that we're all trained to be average — that we pretty much end up being average managers.

But now I'm going to talk about **how each of us is unique!**

Wait! That's confusing!

You just made an argument in the previous book that we're all the same and now you're going to say that we're unique?

Exactly!

There are obvious reasons why **each of us is unique...**

We have different personalities — some of us are low-key, others view being inspiring as our strength, some of us are more driven, and others are more approachable.

In addition, we have different skills and knowledge...

like budgeting, running a team of machine tool operators, or being a pilot in charge of a flight crew on a commercial airliner...

All of which, without question, **make each of us different.**

However, while all of these unique characteristics make us different from one another,

there is **one unique characteristic that's true across every one of us...**

and it's true whether we think we're a fabulous manager or if we are struggling and **aren't a great manager:**

Each of us knows our job better than anyone else!

Repeat: Each of us knows our job better than anyone else!

Think about it.

Do you think your boss knows your job?

If he/she had to step in and do the work you do or the work that I do, most of us would say, with perhaps an exception of two, that **the person we report to would not be able to do our jobs...**

And the reason is that our bosses — whether yours or mine — really don't know what we do.

And if that's the case,

if someone wants to know how you manage, or supervise or do your job as the CEO,

there's no one better to ask than you!

THEN ANOTHER INSIGHT...

While it's good that we are the ones to turn to because we know our jobs the best,

I then had **some sobering thoughts** that followed:

Just as **no one knows your** job as well as you do and your boss can't do your job,

do you really know the jobs of each of the people who is in your group?

Can you do their jobs?

Just as your boss would struggle to do your job...

because he/she doesn't know what you do every day,

isn't it likely that you would also struggle

doing the job of someone reporting to you...

because you don't know what that person has to do every day?

So, following from not knowing the jobs of those who

work for us...

again, the parallel to our bosses not being able to do our jobs,

I had this next thought which prompted a rethinking about the way most of us manage —which, if it is correct,

can move us from being at best average to **highly effective!**

As we all know, in the standard approach to managing that we've all learned, one of the main underlying but unstated ideas about what managers do...

is that when you're the manager — or a supervisor or an executive — **you are in charge.**

Every boss I've worked for over the years thinks this way...

It's just **one of the long-standing** norms in organizational life — the way things are.

"I'm in charge because I — and those who put me in this job, think that I should be... And, as **I obviously know something** or a lot of things that others don't,

I know best,

and, in knowing the best, I'm therefore **the one best-suited to lead** and manage and to make decisions that gets results."

However, is this idea that someone is in charge because the person knows better/best **really on target?**

While some of you may answer "yes,"

that you do know "better" — that **you can make better** decisions... and have greater insight as to what is to be done — and even how to do it,

think back to that question posed a few pages earlier.

Can you do the job of someone reporting to you?

Even if some of us would say that we can… if that question is somewhat representative of how we can demonstrate that we "know better" — then here's **the tougher question:**

Would you then extend that and say that you can also do the jobs… of two perhaps even three or more individuals who are employees in your office or work group?

Can you do the jobs of all of them better than all of them combined?

Of course, you can't.

If you could, you could do all of their work and **you wouldn't need them.**

Now, I know what you're thinking... The reason you need them is because there's so much work to do... that you by yourself can't do it all — even though you know more and have more skills and/or knowledge.

But here's what I concluded:

The reason **we can't do** the jobs of everyone and can't do them better than all of them combined is... because **we really don't know** the detail of the work they do...

just as your boss doesn't know the detail of your work!

And therefore, as managers, don't we have to accept the fact that **they know a heck of a lot —**

and that, despite my believing I'm in charge — I really don't know their jobs better than they do.

That if it is the case for them to do their work every day, **they really do know better** — they have to know their jobs better than I ever would...

because if they didn't,

and because — whether it's you or me — we don't know their jobs well enough to do in their jobs,

things wouldn't get done.

So, just as you **know your job better** than your boss,

and those who work with and for me/you also know more about what needs to be done and how to do it better than any of us as managers will ever know...

shouldn't we accept that how we've been trained and learned to manage doesn't really work?

While these insights helped me enormously as a manager... turning me around,

there is **one final piece** we need to talk about — an important piece that gets to the **challenge of managing effectively.**

Just as your boss doesn't know your job...

and you don't know the jobs of the people who work with and for you...

do you think those who **work for you know your job?**

Repeat: Do you think **they know your job?**

The answer is... not likely!

Because we're in charge and we know best, how **could they possibly know** or understand what we do?

So, here's what all of this leads to:

When you don't know the job of the person you report to... and that person doesn't know your job...

and when you don't know the jobs of the people who work with and for you

and the people working with and for you don't know your job,

it's pretty likely that what we are doing is going to be sub-optimal...

that we're not going to do a good job individually and as a group!

So, **if collectively we** don't really know what each other is doing, can we say, as the managers who "are in charge" **that we are managing well?**

If you find it difficult to explain your job...

because we have so longed relied upon the conventional wisdom...

that a manager (or a supervisor or an executive) is in charge and knows best,

and that therefore the people who work with and for you

most **certainly don't need** to know what you do or have the knowledge of skill to do your job, the reality is that **they can't know** your job.

So, once again, **because they don't know** your job, can you expect them to really do what you think is important?

Now, I know many of us would say.

"They'll know what's important **because I will tell** them what I have decided is important for them to do."

But knowing that the standard management practice of organizing and directing by and large **has generated average results,**

what is the likelihood that this assumption of being in charge, where you plan and organize and tell others what you think is important

and where how you've been trained results in your being average —

is going to lead to **astounding success?**

And when you have sat back and thought about all of the above...

1. that I know my job better than anyone else,

2. that my boss can't do my job because s/he doesn't know what I do every day,

3. that I don't know the jobs of people who work for me,

4. and that the people who report to me don't know my job...

can you still say that you know better?

That you are as effective a manager as you could be?

Page for Notes

Page for Notes

Page for Notes

www.ingramcontent.com/pod-product-compliance
Lightning Source LLC
Chambersburg PA
CBHW030649220526
45463CB00005B/1701